TELEPHONE COURTESY & CUSTOMER SERVICE

Lloyd Finch

CRISP PUBLICATIONS, INC.
Los Altos, California

TELEPHONE COURTESY
& CUSTOMER SERVICE

CREDITS
Editor: **Michael Crisp**
Designer: **Carol Harris**
Typesetting: **Interface Studio**
Cover Design: **Carol Harris**
Artwork: **Ralph Mapson**

Copyright © 1987 by Crisp Publications, Inc.
Printed in the United States of America

Crisp books are distributed in Canada by Reid Publishing, Ltd., P.O. Box 7267, Oakville, Ontario, Canada L6J 6L6.

In Australia by Career Builders, P.O. Box 1051 Springwood, Brisbane, Queensland, Australia 4127.

And in New Zealand by Career Builders, P.O. Box 571, Manurewa, New Zealand.

Library of Congress Catalog Card Number 86-71573
Finch, Lloyd
Telephone Courtesy & Customer Service
ISBN 0-931961-18-1

PREFACE

Welcome to **Telephone Courtesy and Customer Service.** You have been selected for this training because your manager feels you are an important provider of customer service for your organization.

This book has been written so that you can complete it in a relatively short time. The important thing is to carefully read the material, understand it, and apply it to your job.

There are four sections in this book. **Section I** provides objectives for the reader, defines a quality customer service provider, and discusses service responsibility. **Section II** discusses telephone techniques and their importance to providing quality service. **Section III** explains customer "wants and needs," and describes the importance of a positive attitude. **Section IV** teaches the reader how to manage "Customer Perceptions".

Keep this book near your work location for reference. By using it regularly you will learn correct telephone techniques and develop the personal skills required to provide the best possible customer service.

Applying the telephone customer service skills in this book will help you become a professional provider of quality customer service. This should be your objective.

Get out your pencil, relax, and enjoy this book.

Happy Reading!

Lloyd Finch

TELEPHONE COURTESY & CUSTOMER SERVICE is divided into four sections. Each section is designed to help you progress toward the goal of providing quality customer service when using the telephone.

The objective of each section is:

Section I — To understand the basics of providing high quality customer service.

Section II — To learn proper telephone techniques.

Section III — To understand the customer.

Section IV — To manage the customer's perception and understand the essential role customer service plays in the success of your company.

The four objectives are interrelated. Good customer service cannot be provided until all four are understood and applied.

Being a professional customer service provider (regardless of your title or position) is an essential key to the ultimate success of any organization. This makes you a very important person.

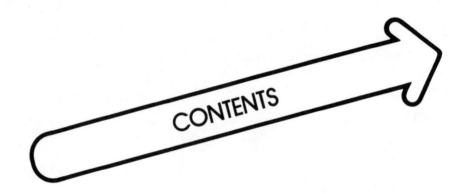

CONTENTS

CONTENTS

SECTION I

QUALITY CUSTOMER SERVICE

Quality customer service is provided by a person like you. A quality customer service provider is a person who:

1. ACCEPTS RESPONSIBILITY FOR PROVIDING TIMELY CUSTOMER SERVICE IN A COURTEOUS MANNER.

2. UNDERSTANDS THAT THE SUCCESS OF AN ORGANIZATION DEPENDS ON GOOD CUSTOMER SERVICE.

3. LEARNS AND PRACTICES CUSTOMER SERVICE SKILLS IN A POSITIVE MANNER.

Often employees are so busy there is little time to think about their jobs or how they relate to the overall success of the company. Sometimes, those who spend much of their day on the telephone talking with outsiders don't consider their jobs to be very important. The fact is, that anyone regularly involved with customer contact has one of the most important jobs in that organization. Following are some points to consider:

- THE SUCCESS OF A COMPANY DEPENDS ON CUSTOMERS. THESE CUSTOMERS WILL NOT RETURN UNLESS THEY ARE TREATED PROFESSIONALLY AND IN A COURTEOUS MANNER.

- MANAGERS NORMALLY TALK WITH ONLY A FEW CUSTOMERS EACH WEEK. OTHER EMPLOYEES TALK WITH DOZENS EACH DAY.

- ANYONE DEALING DIRECTLY WITH CUSTOMERS OCCUPIES A POSITION OF TRUST.

- COMPANIES WITH REPUTATIONS FOR OUTSTANDING SERVICE WERE BUILT OVER TIME, BY PEOPLE LIKE YOU.

CUSTOMER SERVICE IS EVERYONE'S RESPONSIBILITY

When we think about customer service it is common to think that certain individuals or departments are the only ones responsible for providing that service. However, in most organizations customer service departments represent only a portion of the overall service responsibility. Everyone, from president to clerk provides customer service, and as such contributes to a company's reputation for service and courtesy.

If all employees learned to provide the service concepts presented in this book, the reputation of that company with customers would be considered "excellent".

In the next few pages, you will learn about telephone techniques to help you become more professional when you are on the phone with customers and clients.

Learning good techniques and skills is essential; but not as important as applying what has been learned on a daily basis.

QUESTION: DAVE IS A LOBBY RECEPTIONIST FOR ACME SYSTEMS INC. HIS RESPONSIBILITIES INCLUDE REGISTERING AND PROVIDING SECURITY BADGES FOR ALL NON-EMPLOYEES WHO ENTER THE BUILDING. IS DAVE RESPONSIBLE FOR CUSTOMER SERVICE?

ANSWER: YOU BET!

THE IMPORTANCE OF THE TELEPHONE IN YOUR ORGANIZATION

Think for a moment about the role of the telephone where you work. Chances are it would be difficult to conduct business without it. Although there are salespeople and other representatives who meet face to face with customers to generate business, the telephone is probably responsible for most customer contacts.

On an average day, do you know what portion of your customers receive service over the telephone as compared to being contacted in person by a representative of your company? Although companies differ, it is not unusual to have more than 80% of customer contact provided by telephone.

If your company happens to be one where a majority of customer contact is by telephone; do you know who is primarily responsible for the company's customer service reputation? (check one)

_____ Those who meet face to face with the customer?

_____ Those who talk with customers on the telephone?

_____ Managers and supervisors?

> The best answer is those who use the telephone.

Having answered this, who then in your opinion is responsible for providing good customer service? (check all that apply)

_____ Me _____ the managers _____ the sales department

_____ officers of the Company _____ our telephone receptionists

_____ our clerks _____ the delivery people _____ our outside service people

_____ the technical support staff _____ others

> If you checked all of the choices, you get an "A". The most important check mark however belongs next to the word "Me"!

DIAGRAM OF A QUALITY CONSCIOUS COMPANY

The diagram below illustrates how a customer is viewed by the best customer service companies.

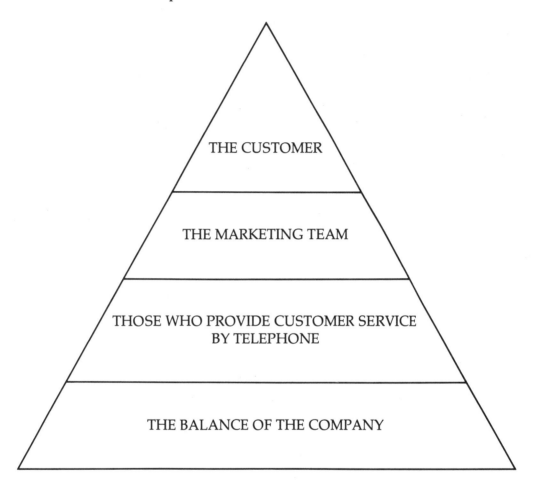

Please notice that the customer is at the top of the PYRAMID but supported by marketing and sales and dependent on the rest of the company to give them the attention they deserve. Keep this diagram in mind as you learn about telephone techniques that can help provide quality customer service.

SECTION II

PROPER TELEPHONE TECHNIQUES

Proper Telephone Techniques are essential to provide quality customer service. In the following pages you will learn the most important telephone techniques. How effectively you use them is up to you.

TELEPHONE TECHNIQUE ONE: HANDLING THE TELEPHONE

Features of the telephone need to be understood. These features are designed to help you handle calls smoothly. At first glance they may seem complicated but normally are easy to use. To better understand the capabilities of your telephone read about the available features, and/or ask a more experienced person to explain them to you. Then practice until they become automatic.

> Joan needed to transfer a caller to a co-worker. She wasn't sure how to do it. After quickly reading the instructions Joan made the transfer. The caller was disconnected. If Joan had spent a few minutes practicing the call transfer feature, the disconnect would not have occured.

- The time to learn about your telephone is ahead of time. Don't practice on the caller. Be familar with all of the features.

- Hold the transmitter portion of the telephone directly in front of your mouth. If the transmitter is held away from your mouth you risk not being understood.

> Keep in mind that speaking on the telephone requires better articulation than is necessary in face to face conversations.

- Place the telephone on your desk so the receiver will be picked up without banging into anything. No one likes unnecessary noise.

- Avoid side conversations while talking on the telephone. Your party deserves your full attention. Do not attempt to carry on two conversations at the same time.

HANDLING THE TELEPHONE (continued)

- Make sure the caller is placed on hold before discussing his or her situation with a co-worker.

> Wouldn't it be embarassing if you told a co-worker that a caller didn't sound too smart, only to discover that he/she was listening?

- Never eat or drink while talking. If your mouth is full when the telephone rings, wait a few seconds before answering.

- Answer in as few rings as possible. A maximum of three rings is a good standard.

> Some organizations have a ''Three Ring Policy''. Check to see if yours does.

- When you place a caller on hold to answer another line; ask for permission and WAIT FOR AN ANSWER.

> **EXAMPLE:** Would you mind holding while I answer my other line? Wait for the customer to say; ''Sure go ahead.'' Too often you hear; ''please hold'' and the person is gone.

- If you have several callers on hold, remember the priority of each call. If necessary, make notes of who is holding and on which line.

> Nothing is more irritating than to answer the question, ''Who are your holding for?'' several times.

TELEPHONE TECHNIQUE TWO:

YOUR VOICE INFLECTION

Try this inflection exercise by speaking into a tape recorder.

Read the following sentence in your normal voice:

"Jimmy didn't show up for work this morning."

Now restate the same sentence with "surprise" in your voice.

Try it again, but this time make it a "casual" statement.

Next, make it sound like a "secret".

Finally, turn it into a "question".

If done properly, as your inflection changes, the sentence will convey a completely different meaning to the listener.

TELEPHONE TECHNIQUE THREE: YOUR BEST VOICE

We all have voices that sound different. Some of us have the deep voice of authority, while others of us sound meek or frail. Voices can be pleasant or annoying; easy to decipher or unintelligible; clear as a bell or squeaky. The voice you project is determined by four factors; all of which can be controlled.

ENERGY—The energy in your voice reflects your attitude and enthusiam.

RATE OF SPEECH—A normal rate is 125 words a minute. Speaking faster can create problems.

PITCH—This can be a monotone, a low, or a high pitch. Ideally you should vary your tone and inflection.

QUALITY—The above three factors make up your voice quality.

There are several things you can do to produce a more desirable speaking voice. Some include:

1. Warm up by humming a song. This will help deepen the sound of your voice.

2. Practicing your pitch and control by calling a telephone recording device and delivering several messages. Then listen to the playback and critique yourself or ask a friend to help.

3. Role play with a friend, and tape record the conversation. Review it for tone, rate of delivery, etc. . . .

4. Take a speech class in a local college or extension program to learn some voice exercises to help you avoid a monotone sound.

5. PUT A SMILE INTO YOUR VOICE. It's easy to do. Simply remember to smile as you answer a call. Believe it or not, your voice will sound friendlier.

VOICE SELF-ASSESSMENT

Your voice reflects your personality. If it needs improvement you can do it, but you must be willing to try. Practicing voice techniques is no different than practicing a sport. If you stay at it, you're bound to improve.

Rate your voice using the following self evaluation. Check those characteristics that apply to you, and then ask a friend to help evaluate your responses.

MY VOICE:

DESIRABLE TRAITS		UNDESIRABLE TRAITS	
is pleasant sounding	____	is nasal	____
has pitch variations	____	sounds throaty	____
has a normal rate	____	is raspy	____
varies in volume	____	sometimes squeaks	____
has distinct articulation	____	is a boring monotone	____
sounds like I am smiling	____	is too weak	____
has ample force	____	is too loud	____
stresses proper accents	____	has too many pauses	____
		does not convey a "smile"	____

For any undesirable traits checked, you should begin work on correcting them. The techniques suggested in this book should help, but you may also need to enroll in a speech improvement class so an expert can diagnose and prescribe appropriate voice exercises.

TELEPHONE TECHNIQUE FOUR: ADDRESSING THE CALLER

Rules about how to address callers can be confusing because of the many options. Therefore the following may help.

> There are seven basic ways to address a calling party.
>
> Mr. Mrs. Miss Ms. First Name Sir and Ma'am

The average caller may or may not be sensitive about how he or she is addressed. To be on the safe side keep these suggestions in mind:

1. When addressing a male you are always correct to use Mr. or Sir.

2. Addressing a woman is more confusing. The use of Mrs. or Miss is common and generally acceptable. Some women prefer Ms. and may request this form of address. If you are uncertain, simply ask the caller for her preference, (i.e. Shall I address you as Miss or Mrs? Is it Mrs. or Miss? Is it Miss. or Ms. Taylor?).

3. Often when you ask for the correct form of address the caller will suggest the use of a first name. The use of the customer's first name is then acceptable. Use of a first name may also be acceptable (but not always) when:

   • You have established a good rapport over a period of time.

   • You have been called by your first name.

   • You know the caller, and know he/she is comfortable with a first name basis.

TELEPHONE TECHNIQUE FIVE: ANSWERING THE TELEPHONE

A caller will begin to mentally measure the quality of the organization before they hear a voice by the number of rings it takes to get an answer. The next impression comes with the first voice they hear. Imagine a cheerful "Good Morning, Jones Enterprises" verus a terse clipped "International Widget, please hold."

The rules for answering a telephone are simple but they need to be continually reviewed and practiced. Following are the most basic ones which should always be employed.

1. Use the four answering courtesies:
   - Greet the caller
   - State your organization (or department)
   - Introduce yourself
   - Offer your help

   > EXAMPLE: GOOD AFTERNOON, ACCOUNTING, MARY JONES SPEAKING. HOW MAY I HELP YOU?

2. Be enthusiastic when you answer. Help make the calling party feel truly welcome.

   > A TIRED VOICE LACKING IN ENTHUSIAM IS UNAPPEALING.

3. Use friendly phrases as part of your greeting.

   > SUCH AS: THANKS FOR CALLING
   >   MAY I HELP YOU?
   >   HOW ARE YOU TODAY?

4. Remember to smile as you pick up the receiver.

   > IDEA: TAPE THE WORD SMILE ON YOUR RECEIVER

TELEPHONE TECHNIQUE
SIX: EFFECTIVE LISTENING:

The first lesson in listening is to be aware that there are only three types of expressions you hear from callers. They will:

1. MAKE STATEMENTS

2. OFFER OBJECTIONS, or

3. ASK QUESTIONS

Similarily, there are three things that can happen when you fail to listen closely.

1. YOU WILL HEAR WHAT YOU WANT TO HEAR

2. YOU WILL HEAR WHAT YOU EXPECT TO HEAR

3. YOU WILL NOT RECOGNIZE THE DIFFERENCE BETWEEN A STATEMENT, OBJECTION, OR QUESTION.

If you do not listen closely you may not be able to understand what the call is about. For example:

CUSTOMER STATEMENT: "YOUR PRICES ARE A LITTLE HIGHER THAN I THOUGHT THEY WOULD BE."

Close your eyes and imagine a customer making this remark. How would you interpret it?
(check one)

_____ THE CUSTOMER HAS AN OBJECTION.

_____ THE CUSTOMER MADE A STATEMENT.

_____ THE CUSTOMER HAS ASKED A QUESTION.

Answer: The customer was making a statement

EFFECTIVE LISTENING (continued)

Let's see how Helen, a professional service representative, would respond to the statement on the previous page.

CUSTOMER:	"YOUR PRICES ARE A LITTLE HIGHER THAN I THOUGHT THEY WOULD BE."
HELEN:	"I HOPE THAT WON'T BE A PROBLEM. THEY ARE EXCELLENT PRODUCTS. MAY I HAVE YOUR BILLING ADDRESS?"

Helen acknowledged the statement and then moved the conversation to the next step. If Helen had not been listening closely she might have misinterpreted the statement as an objection or a question. For example suppose Helen had interpreted the customer's statement as an objection. Her response might have gone like this.

"CUSTOMER:	YOUR PRICES ARE A LITTLE HIGHER THAN I THOUGHT THEY WOULD BE."
HELEN:	"OUR PRICES ARE VERY COMPETITIVE, IN FACT WE LOWERED SOME PRICES THIS YEAR."
CUSTOMER:	"THEY SEEM HIGH TO ME."
HELEN:	"IF YOU COMPARED OUR PRICES WITH OUR COMPETITORS YOU WOULD FIND THAT ON THE AVERAGE WE ARE VERY COMPETITIVE."
CUSTOMER:	"WHO ARE YOUR MAJOR COMPETITORS?"

In this example, Helen allowed the conversation to become a discussion regarding prices and competitors. Helen lost control simply because she handled a statement as if it were an objection.

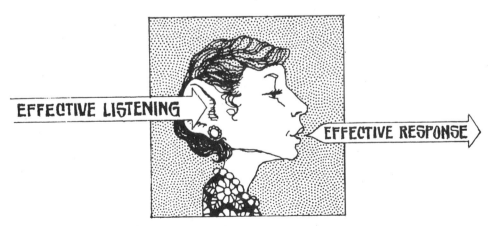

TELEPHONE TECHNIQUE SEVEN: MANAGING OBJECTIONS

An objection occurs when the caller is opposed to the proposed plan of action. When you hear an objection it is important to address it immediately. If the caller offers an objection and you ignore it, you may have lost a customer.

EXAMPLE:

CUSTOMER:	(OBJECTION) "YOUR PRICES SEEM HIGH AND I THINK I SHOULD SHOP AROUND AND COMPARE PRICES BEFORE I PLACE MY ORDER."
DOUG:	"I AM SURE THAT YOU WILL BE SATISFIED WITH OUR PRODUCT. WILL A FRIDAY DELIVERY DATE BE OKAY?"

In this example Doug was not listening. He did not hear the customer's objection and as a result tried to move the sale along. Doug deserves credit for trying to get the order but there is not much point when the customer's objection goes unanswered.

Most of us do not like objections. We sometimes think that if objections are ignored they will go away. They won't. Objections require an immediate reply.

EXAMPLE:

CUSTOMER:	(OBJECTION) "I THINK I SHOULD COMPARE PRICES BEFORE PLACING AN ORDER."
HELEN:	"THAT'S FINE. OUR CUSTOMERS TELL US WE ARE VERY PRICE COMPETITIVE. WE RECENTLY LOWERED PRICES ON THE MODEL YOU ARE CONSIDERING, AND IT CONTINUES TO CARRY THE BEST WARRANTY IN THE INDUSTRY. IF YOU PLACE YOUR ORDER NOW WE COULD DELIVER IT EARLY NEXT WEEK."

MANAGING OBJECTIONS (continued)

If you ignore objections or questions a caller will usually:

1. Stop you and repeat the objection or the question.

2. Not say anything to you but still be dissatisfied because you ignored them.

When listening always pay attention to voice inflection. It communicates a great deal. Suppose the customer says "Your delivery dates are unbelievable". If the customer made this statement in an assertive voice you would interpret it as an objection. If delivered in a cheerful voice the customer has probably paid a compliment. Callers will let you know when they object to something, and their objections will usually be direct and to the point. Your job is to listen closely.

SUMMARY: MANAGING OBJECTIONS

1. Listen to what the caller says.

2. Always provide an immediate response.

3. State the response in clear and positive terms.

4. Do not provide unnecessary information and conversation.

On the following page is an exercise to help you learn to distinguish between statements, questions and objections. This activity should help you to become a more sensitive listener.

EXERCISE AHEAD

STATEMENTS, QUESTIONS OR OBJECTIONS?

In the following exercise read each expression as if it has just been delivered to you on the telephone. Then write an "S" if you think it is a STATEMENT, a "Q" if you think it is a QUESTION, and an "O" for those you think are OBJECTIONS. For expressions that are both questions and objections, write both letters in order of your ranking.

Assume all responses have been made in a normal tone of voice, (you will notice that all punctuation has purposely been left out).

1. _____ I THINK YOUR SERVICE IS QUITE GOOD

2. _____ YOUR DELIVERY DATES ARE CERTAINLY LONG ENOUGH

3. _____ WHY DOES THE BILL SHOW $107.00 DOLLARS

4. _____ YOUR PRICES ARE JUST TOO HIGH FOR ME

5. _____ YOU DON'T UNDERSTAND. I NEED SOMEONE OUT HERE TODAY

6. _____ WHEN WILL IT BE IN STOCK

7. _____ WHAT ARE YOU GOING TO DO ABOUT THE BACK ORDER

8. _____ I CAN'T WAIT. I NEED TO TALK WITH HER TODAY

9. _____ WHY IS HE NEVER AROUND WHEN I NEED HIM

10 _____ I AM NOT GOING TO PAY THAT BILL

(Answers are at the bottom of this page)

ANSWERS: 1. STATEMENT
2. OBJECTION, STATEMENT
3. QUESTION
4. OBJECTION
5. OBJECTION
6. QUESTION
7. QUESTION
8. OBJECTION
9. OBJECTION, QUESTION
10. OBJECTION

TELEPHONE TECHNIQUE EIGHT: THE ART OF NEGOTIATION*

Often you will have to negotiate with a customer. Negotiating involves recognizing the needs of the caller, comparing them against your organization's ability to deliver what is required, and then reaching a solution that will satisfy both parties. Negotiation is required when a request is made for service you cannot or do not offer.

Negotiation begins with "ACTION ISSUES". These are concerns or requests that need to be met in order to satisfy the caller.

Successful negotiation does not mean offering a service your company can not provide. Instead it means the ability to reach a compromise that is acceptable to both your organization and the caller.

To illustrate some negotiation techniques let's listen in on a conversation between Jane and a customer.

CUSTOMER:	"This is Bob Martin calling. I must speak with Mrs. Sims right now."
JANE:	"I'm sorry Sir but she is on another call. May I help you or take your telephone number and have her call you back?"
CUSTOMER:	"No, I can't wait. Interrupt her and let her know that I must speak to her."

Jane has an assertive customer who is demanding to talk with Mrs. Sims.

Jane knows that Mrs. Sims is already on an important call and does not want to be interrupted.

In this situation there is a conflict between what the customer wants and what Jane can provide. Usually, in this type of situation there is room for negotiation.

If you were confronted with this situation what would you do to provide a compromise the customer would accept?

(continued on next page)

*For an excellent book on Negotiation see the order form in the back of the book.

THE ART OF NEGOTIATION (continued)

HERE ARE SOME TIPS:

1. Ask questions to determine the problem.

2. When you select a course of action, be direct and specific in your statements

3. Remain positive and service oriented.

If you were Jane how would you respond to the customer?

THE CUSTOMER SAYS: "No, I can't wait. Interrupt and let her know that I must speak to her."

Write your response. (Keep the above guideline in mind)

YOUR RESPONSE: _____

_____

_____

_____

_____

_____

_____

(Read the facing page to see how Jane negotiated with the customer.)

THE ART OF NEGOTIATION (continued)

CUSTOMER:	"NO, I CAN'T WAIT. INTERRUPT AND LET HER KNOW THAT I MUST SPEAK WITH HER."
JANE:	"SIR, I'M SURE MRS. SIMS WOULD LIKE TO TALK TO YOU, BUT SINCE SHE IS NOT AVAILABLE, PLEASE EXPLAIN WHAT YOU NEED AND I'LL EITHER PERSONALLY TAKE CARE OF IT OR FIND SOMEONE TO HELP YOU. WILL THAT BE ALL RIGHT?"
CUSTOMER:	"WELL, MAYBE YOU CAN HELP. OUR SYSTEM HAS BEEN DOWN FOR ABOUT TWO HOURS?"
JANE:	"DID YOU CALL OUR SERVICE DEPARTMENT"
CUSTOMER:	"YES I DID."
JANE:	"WHAT DID THEY SAY?"
CUSTOMER:	"ONE OF YOUR TECHNICIANS WAS TO HAVE BEEN HERE BY TEN O'CLOCK. HE HAS NOT SHOWN UP. I CAN'T REACH YOUR SERVICE DEPARTMENT BECAUSE THE LINES ARE CONSTANTLY BUSY."
JANE:	"I'LL CALL THE SERVICE DEPARTMENT AND FIND OUT WHAT THEY ARE DOING ABOUT YOUR PROBLEM. WILL YOU HOLD FOR A MOMENT?"
CUSTOMER:	"OKAY."

(JANE CALLS THE SERVICE DEPARTMENT AND
LEARNS THE TECHNICIAN WAS DELAYED AT
ANOTHER LOCATION AND WILL NOT BE AT MR.
MARTINS FOR ANOTHER HOUR).

JANE:	"MR. MARTIN I TALKED WITH THE SUPERVISOR IN THE CUSTOMER SERVICE DEPARTMENT AND SHE SAID YOUR TECHNICIAN HAS BEEN DELAYED BUT WILL BE THERE WITHIN THE HOUR. I WILL CHECK BACK REGULARLY TO MAKE CERTAIN THE TECHNICIAN WILL GO DIRECTLY TO YOUR COMPANY TO MEET HIS NEW DEADLINE. I WILL ALSO INFORM MRS. SIMS THAT YOU CALLED. WILL THAT BE ALL RIGHT?"
CUSTOMER:	"I GUESS SO."
JANE:	"THANKS FOR YOUR PATIENCE MR. MARTIN."
CUSTOMER:	"OKAY, THANKS FOR YOUR HELP."

THE ART OF NEGOTIATION (continued)

REVIEW

Obviously, the customer is not completely satisfied. He would like the technician to be at his business immediately, but since this is not possible, an alternate plan was arranged and he has agreed to it. Let's review Jane's course of action.

1. She raised her voice slightly to become more assertive.

2. By asking questions, she learned what the customer needed.

3. She proposed a course of action.

4. She was direct and specific in her statements.

In most service situations, an acceptable compromise can be reached through negotiation. Since you control the service, you are in a position to suggest a compromise or make another arrangement. In Jane's situation she had two ACTION ISSUES to deal with.

The customer demanded to speak with Mrs. Sims.

The customer wanted a technician immediately.

Jane knew Mrs. Sims was not available. She also knew she would not be able to get the technician to the customer's location immediately. Despite this, she took positive action, presented a plan, and asked that the customer accept it.

When you control service you must be careful with your statements to avoid coming on too strong. Even though you cannot always provide what the customer wants, it is important to deliver the response in a courteous manner.

TELEPHONE TECHNIQUE NINE: THE SERVICE FOLLOW-UP CALL

Following up on the service you provide is professional. In the situation you just read, Jane or Mrs. Sims should follow up with Mr. Martin to see if he is satisfied. Many customer service providers do not regularly follow up. They claim they do not have time. Even when it is impossible to follow up with every customer, there are certain situations where it should be done. A few examples include:

1. NOTHING WENT RIGHT.   Sometimes you have a situation where despite everyone's best effort, nothing goes right. Once the problems have been corrected the customer should be called to determine whether everything is now satisfactory. The customer will usually appreciate this courtesy.

2. THE IRATE CUSTOMER.   When you hang up from a conversation with an irate customer, the last thing you want to do is speak with that customer again. Whether the cause of the complaint was legitimate, or questionable, a follow-up call is a good idea. By calling to ask if the action you initiated was satisfactory, the customer will be pleasantly surprised to hear from you, and perhaps will become a good customer.

3. A NEW CUSTOMER.   When you establish a new account or provide service to a new customer, it's a good time to extend an extra courtesy. Make a follow-up call to learn if everything is satisfactory. The customer's perception of your company will be enhanced, and repeat business may be likely.

4. THE REGULAR CUSTOMER.   Those who do business with you deserve occasional follow up calls. It is easy to take regular customers for granted. An occasional friendly follow-up service call tells regular customers ''we care about you.''

Never hesitate to make a follow up service call. Even when the customer was irate, or the service you provided did not go as planned, call. It is always better to know the level of customer satisfaction than guess at it. If a customer continues to have a problem, you need to know about it so it can be corrected. If there is no longer a problem, the customer will appreciate the follow-up.

TELEPHONE TECHNIQUE TEN: ASKING QUESTIONS:

Often you are required to ask questions to get information you need. There are two types of questions that can be used and each has a particular purpose. The types are, open questions and closed questions.

OPEN QUESTIONS ARE DESIGNED TO OBTAIN ANSWERS THAT CANNOT BE ANSWERED WITH A SIMPLE YES OR NO.

FOR EXAMPLE IF YOU ASK A CUSTOMER, ''DID YOU RECEIVE THE SHIPMENT?''

THE ANSWER WILL BE EITHER YES OR NO.

IF YOU WANTED THE CUSTOMER TO DISCUSS THE PARTICULARS OF THE SHIPMENT YOU COULD ASK INSTEAD:

''WHAT WAS THE CONDITION OF THE SHIPMENT WHEN IT ARRIVED?''

AN EXPLANATION IS REQUIRED

Use OPEN questions when you want a customer to explain or discuss something. CLOSED questions should be used when all you need is a yes or no. Use both types of questions to gain better control of your telephone contacts. It is also possible to shorten telephone calls by effectively using OPEN and CLOSED questions.

At the beginning of most customer calls you need to learn what the customer wants so you would use OPEN questions. Later, you may need to employ CLOSED questions to get the customer's agreement; to understand a service request, or just to manage the conversation and your time.

ASKING QUESTIONS (continued)

Open questions begin with the words
How, Why, When, Who, What, and Where

EXAMPLES OF OPEN QUESTIONS:

- HOW OFTEN DOES THAT HAPPEN?
- WHAT DID YOU DO BEFORE THE PROBLEM STARTED?
- WHO IS RESPONSIBLE FOR YOUR BILLING?
- WHEN DID THE PACKAGE ARRIVE?

Closed questions begin with words like:
Did, Can, Have, Do, Is, Will, and Would

EXAMPLES OF CLOSED QUESTIONS:

- DID YOU CALL THEM?
- DO YOU HAVE YOUR BILL?
- HAVE YOU RECEIVED OUR REFUND?
- WILL YOU ATTEND OUR SEMINAR?
- MAY I DO THAT FOR YOU?

Any statement can be "closed" by following it with a question. For example:

I WOULD LIKE TO SEND YOU A BROCHURE ABOUT OUR PRODUCTS.

WILL THAT BE OKAY?

YOU PROMISED TO CALL ME BACK BY FOUR O'CLOCK. IS THAT CORRECT?

Other examples of closed questions you can use at the end of statements include:

DO YOU APPROVE?
WILL YOU PARTICIPATE?
IS THAT A GOOD TIME TO CALL?
WILL THAT BE ALL RIGHT?

List some of your own in the space below:

_____

_____

_____

_____

ASKING QUESTIONS (continued)

Short closed questions can also be used to obtain the customer's agreement. For example:

> OUR TECHNICIAN WILL BE THERE ON FRIDAY.
> <u>WILL THAT BE OKAY?</u>
>
> WE HAVE TO BILL YOU FOR THAT SERVICE. <u>IS THAT ALL RIGHT?</u>
>
> I WILL CALL YOU 10:00 AM MONDAY MORNING.
> <u>WILL YOU BE AVAILABLE?</u>

These examples sound like you are giving the customer a choice. However, you are basically asking for a confirmation of your statement.

Suppose you were arranging an appointment for one of your sales representatives. The only open date you had to offer was Tuesday at nine o'clock. You could say:

> "I'M SORRY MISS JOHNSON BUT THE ONLY DATE MR. STEVENS HAS OPEN IS TUESDAY AT NINE O'CLOCK. I HOPE THAT WILL BE OKAY."

This statement is poorly phrased. It could be stated more positively if you said:

> "MISS JOHNSON I HAVE ARRANGED FOR OUR SALES REPRESENTATIVE MR. STEVENS TO VISIT YOU ON TUESDAY AT NINE O'CLOCK. WILL THAT BE ALL RIGHT?

The customer might still request a different date however, your statement sounds like you have taken positive action.

EXERCISE AHEAD

ASKING QUESTIONS (continued)

Take a few minutes to complete the following exercise on
OPEN and CLOSED questions. Identify the questions
below as either CLOSED or OPEN. Write a C for CLOSED
questions and an O for the OPEN ones. Answers are on
the next page.

1. _____ What did you do with the disk?

2. _____ Where did the customer's paperwork go?

3. _____ Have you paid the bill?

4. _____ We need the payment by Friday. Will that be okay?

5. _____ How much work is required?

6. _____ Can it be fixed?

7. _____ Is the customer holding?

8. _____ How many calls did we make today?

9. _____ Why did our incoming calls stop at three o'clock?

10. _____ Ms. Jones is happy with our service. Isn't she?

11. _____ Why didn't you test it?

12. _____ Will you call me?

13. _____ How long have you been doing business with us?

14. _____ Do you want to have lunch?

15. _____ Customers are always right. Aren't they?

16. _____ Did the boss tell you to do that?

17. _____ What is the latest inventory level?

18. _____ They were pretty high. Weren't they?

19. _____ Closed questions are answered with a yes or no. Isn't that true?

20. _____ Why do open questions begin with words like how, why, when, where, and what?

ASKING QUESTIONS (continued)

(Answers from page 27)

	KEY WORDS	
	OPEN	**CLOSED**
	HOW	DID
	WHY	CAN
	WHEN	HAVE
	WHO	DO
	WHAT	WILL
	WHERE	IS
		WOULD

QUESTION	ANSWER
1. OPEN	QUESTION BEGINS WITH WHAT
2. OPEN	QUESTION BEGINS WITH WHERE
3. CLOSED	QUESTION BEGINS WITH HAVE
4. CLOSED	ENDS WITH A CLOSED QUESTION
5. OPEN	QUESTION BEGINS WITH HOW
6. CLOSED	QUESTION BEGINS WITH CAN
7. CLOSED	QUESTION BEGINS WITH IS
8. OPEN	QUESTION BEGINS WITH HOW
9. OPEN	QUESTION BEGINS WITH WHY
10. CLOSED	ENDS WITH A CLOSED QUESTION
11. OPEN	QUESTION BEGINS WITH WHY
12. CLOSED	QUESTION BEGINS WITH WILL
13. OPEN	QUESTION BEGINS WITH HOW
14. CLOSED	QUESTION BEGINS WITH DO
15. CLOSED	ENDS WITH A CLOSED QUESTION
16. CLOSED	QUESTION BEGINS WITH DID
17. OPEN	QUESTION BEGINS WITH WHAT
18. CLOSED	ENDS WITH A CLOSED QUESTION
19. CLOSED	ENDS WITH A CLOSED QUESTION
20. OPEN	QUESTION BEGINS WITH WHY

To improve your use of open and closed questions practice is required. Don't you agree? (closed)

ASKING QUESTIONS (continued)

USING QUESTIONS WHEN FACT FINDING

When fact finding keep the following in mind. It will help you determine when to use OPEN or CLOSED questions. You may wish to copy this page and keep it near your phone to remind you when to use OPEN or CLOSED questions.

1. TO DETERMINE PROBLEMS, UNDERSTAND REQUESTS, OR ESTABLISH NEEDS

(USE OPEN QUESTIONS)

2. TO ASK CALLERS TO EXPLAIN REQUESTS OR PROBLEMS

(USE OPEN QUESTIONS)

3. TO ASK FOR MORE INFORMATION TO DETERMINE A COURSE OF ACTION

(USE BOTH OPEN AND CLOSED QUESTIONS)

4. TO GET AGREEMENT

(USE CLOSED QUESTIONS)

SUSAN'S PROBLEM: SUSAN WORKS IN THE MESSSAGE CENTER OF THE COAST CITY BANK. SHE HAS RECEIVED SEVERAL COMPLAINTS ABOUT THE LACK OF INFORMATION SHE OBTAINS FROM CUSTOMERS IN THE MESSAGES SHE TAKES FOR OTHERS. SUSAN COULD IMPROVE HER PERFORMANCE IF SHE FOLLOWED THE ADVICE ABOVE. DON'T YOU AGREE?

TELEPHONE TECHNIQUE ELEVEN: MAKING THE OUTBOUND SERVICE CALL

Anytime you call a customer there are important steps to follow. Even though you may not be calling to sell a product, the basic steps of a successful telemarketing call still apply.

BEFORE YOU MAKE YOUR CALL DEVELOP AN ACTION PLAN.

- GREET THE CUSTOMER IN A FRIENDLY WAY
- INTRODUCE YOURSELF AND YOUR COMPANY
- STATE THE PURPOSE OF THE CALL
- DELIVER YOUR MESSAGE IN FRIENDLY, CLEAR, AND BUSINESS LIKE TERMS, LEAVING ROOM FOR QUESTIONS.
- STATE ANY CUSTOMER BENEFITS
- ASK FOR AGREEMENT

Here's an example:

Cindy mistakenly overbooked a seminar. She needed to call Mrs. Stanger from the Acme Company to explain why the seminar date had to be changed. Cindy developed the following telemarketing action plan.

HER OBJECTIVE: Arrange a new seminar date for the Acme Company.

THE APPROACH: Briefly explain the need for the change and offer two alternate dates.

CUSTOMER BENEFITS: The seminar will be less crowded on the new dates and Acme will receive more attention from the seminar leader.

Cindy called Mrs. Stanger and said: ''Good morning, Mrs. Stanger. This is Cindy Rogers from GAC. How are you today?...The reason for my call is to discuss your seminar date. The date I booked for your group is too crowded. What I can do is offer a date that will be less crowded. This means you will be able to ask more questions and receive more attention from the seminar leader. I have the 16th or 20th available. Do you have a preference?

In the situation above, Cindy did a good job because she turned a negative situation positive by planning ahead.

TELEPHONE TECHNIQUE TWELVE: DELIVERING BAD NEWS

Occasionally you will not be able to provide that which was promised. In these situations it is essential to telephone the customer to explain what has happened. Keeping a customer informed is courteous service. There will be times when it may be unpleasant to deliver ''bad news'' but it must be done.

There are two approaches you can use. We call one the DIRECT APPROACH and the other GOOD NEWS/BAD NEWS.

HERE IS AN EXAMPLE OF THE DIRECT APPROACH:

''Good morning Mr. King. This is Jim West from Woodwinds Unlimited. Do you have a moment? The reason for my call is to let you know that I made a mistake when I added your bill yesterday. I quoted you $287.00 but the correct total is $337.00. I apologize for the error, but wanted to insure the correct amount was okay with you.''

HERE IS THE SAME EXAMPLE USING THE GOOD NEWS/BAD NEWS APPROACH

''Good morning Mr. King. This is Jim West from Woodwinds Unlimited. How are you today? I wanted you to know that I confirmed our technician will visit you on Friday as scheduled. I also wanted you to know that I misquoted the service charge during our last conversation. I quoted a service charge of $125.00 and it's really $150.00. I apologize for the error and hope it won't cause problems.''

When you make an error (and we all do) it is important to accept responsibility for it. Be honest with your customer. No one likes unpleasant surprises such as unexpected billing amounts; people who do not show up; or shipments which differ from what was ordered.

TELEPHONE TECHNIQUE THIRTEEN: RECOGNIZING & MANAGING CALLER BEHAVIOR

Every customer is different. Experienced customer service providers learn to recognize these differences and adjust their behavior accordingly in order to provide better service.

Let's look at three behavior styles callers often demonstrate on the telephone:

CALLER BEHAVIOR PATTERNS
1. ASSERTIVE
2. AGGRESSIVE AND/OR IRATE
3. PASSIVE

MANAGING THE ASSERTIVE CUSTOMER

An assertive person is quick to show authority, and demand action. When you have a telephone contact with an assertive customer, it is important to initially be passive and listen closely to what is said. Once you understand what is needed you should become specific and direct. Normally you do not need to ask an assertive customer many questions because they make it clear what they want. Closed questions will allow you to manage the conversation. Assertive customers are interested in "bottom line" results. When they call and make a request, they expect a fast response.

When dealing with an assertive customer on the telephone you may need to raise your assertiveness level to simply manage the conversation. Sometimes it is difficult to build rapport with an assertive caller because they may not be interested in exchanging pleasantries. It is important not to take this lack of rapport personally.

SUMMARY: HOW TO RESPOND TO AN ASSERTIVE CALLER.
1. Be passive and listen until you understand the problem or request.
2. Be friendly, but specific and direct in your statements.
3. Use closed questions to manage the conversation.
4. If your voice is soft, raise it slightly.
5. Don't get upset if you have difficulty establishing rapport. Responsive service will satisfy the assertive customer.

MANAGING CALLER BEHAVIOR (continued)

MANAGING AN AGGRESSIVE, IRATE CALLER

Managing an irate aggressive customer is difficult. If done properly however, it can be rewarding. Professional telephone service representatives often manage aggressive callers to the point where they actually become friendly.

When you have a telephone contact with an irate customer diffuse his or her complaint. This is done by offering understanding and sympathy, not by arguing.

EXAMPLES:

> "Mrs. Smiley, I understand how you must feel."
>
> "Mr. Welch I don't blame you for being upset. Let's see if we can correct the problem."

When the customer has a legitimate complaint the best thing to do is agree.

EXAMPLES:

> "Mrs. Johnson you are right. You were promised a callback yesterday and you weren't called. Let's start again and get this problem solved."
>
> "I'm sorry Mr. Valdez, I promised you delivery by yesterday and didn't make it. This time I promise we'll do it right."

When a customer complains, offer your concern that they are upset, but don't take aggressive or hostile comments personally.

EXAMPLES:

> "I'm sorry you are upset and I understand your problem. Let me personally check for you. Will you hold for a moment?"
>
> "I'm sorry that you are not satisfied with our service. What can I do to help the situation?"

MANAGING CALLER BEHAVIOR (continued)

SUMMARY: TELEPHONE TECHNIQUES FOR MANAGING THE IRATE AGGRESSIVE CUSTOMER

1. Sympathize and offer understanding.

2. Agree with the customer if they are right.

3. Promise to take corrective action and then do it!

4. Advise the customer of your actions.

5. Remain courteous and provide assurance.

THE PASSIVE CUSTOMER

Passive customers are usually easy to manage and service. Satisfied customers are often passive. Experience has told them they do not need to push or complain. They know they will receive the service they need.

In many telephone contacts a customer may switch from being aggressive or assertive to passive. When this happens it may be a signal the customer is satisfied with the service they are receiving.

Monitor a few of your telephone conversations to determine how often this happens. Most customers do not want to have to take an aggressive stance to get good service. They simply want service that is "hassle" free.

TELEPHONE TECHNIQUE FOURTEEN: MANAGING THE CUSTOMER CALLBACK

When you are unable to handle a request at the time of the original telephone call here are four callback steps to follow:

1. BRIEFLY EXPLAIN THE NEED FOR THE CALLBACK

2. ASK FOR PERMISSION TO MAKE A CALLBACK

3. MAKE A COMMITMENT TO CALL AT AN AGREED UPON TIME

4. PERSONALIZE YOUR STATEMENTS.

Here is an example of how to manage a customer callback:

> "IT WILL TAKE SOME TIME TO GET THAT INFORMATION FOR YOU MR. JONES. WILL IT BE OKAY IF I CALL YOU BACK THIS AFTERNOON BEFORE FOUR O'CLOCK?

If we break this statement into the four callback steps it would look like this:

> **1.** It will take some time **(explaining the need for the callback)** to get that information for you **2.** Mr. Jones. **(personalized). 3.** Will it be okay **(asking permission)** if I call you back this afternoon **4.** before four o'clock? **(commitment)**

Another example:

> "Mrs. Jones, it's going to take a while because I want to completely research the material for you. I won't be able to call you back until tomorrow morning at 10:00 am. Will that be all right?"

Remember, customers expect a fast response. When you cannot provide one you need to commit to an action plan, including the time you will call back. Be sure to offer a return call time that you can meet. Don't compound your problem by committing to an unrealistic deadline.

TELEPHONE TECHNIQUE FIFTEEN: SOME STATEMENTS TO AVOID

Often unknowingly, employees make a telephone statement that will leave customers with negative perceptions. Following are some of those common telephone statements.

(CHECK THOSE STATEMENTS YOU HAVE HEARD OR USED YOURSELF)

1. _____ I'm sorry. Mrs. Jones is still at lunch.

2. _____ I don't know where he is, may I take your number and have him call you?

3. _____ I think she is still having coffee. I'll have her call you.

4. _____ She is in the middle of a big customer problem. Would you like to leave a message?

5. _____ He is at the doctor's office.

6. _____ She went home early.

7. _____ I'm sorry Mr. Smith has not come in yet.

8. _____ The service person should be there on Friday.

9. _____ Your bill should be correct now.

10. _____ Our service department takes forever to answer the phone.

The facing page contains an evaluation of these "too common" statements.

SOME STATEMENTS TO AVOID (continued)

1. "I'm sorry. Mrs. Jones is still at lunch."
The key word is "still". Saying "still" implies a long lunch hour.

2. "I don't know where he is, may I take your number and have him call you?"
You hear this a lot. When there is a call for someone, and you are not sure where the person is, that information should not be shared with the caller. A simple "He is unavailable at the moment, may I have him call you?" will do fine.

3. "I think she is still having coffee. I'll have her call you."
Similar to question one and two. This information need not be shared with the customer.

4. "She is in the middle of a big customer problem."
This statement tells your caller that you have "big customer problems". Why share this type of information? Simply say; "I'm sorry she is unavailable and offer to take a message or to help the caller.

5. "He is at the doctor's office."
Do not share personal information about a co-worker with the customer. Instead, say: "He will be out of the office until three o'clock. May I help you?"

6. "She went home early."
Customers get furious at this one. They need help and discover the person who can help them went home early. Treat this situation as personal information and do not share it.

7. "I'm sorry but Mr. Smith has not come in yet."
The word yet implies being late. Just say: "I am sorry but Mr. Smith is not available. May I help you?"

8. "Our service person should be there on Friday."
Keep statements positive. Avoid creating doubts about your service. Change "should be there" to "will be there".

9. "Your bill should be correct now."
Words like "should" as compared to "will" make your statement negative. Use positive words.

10. "The service department takes forever to answer the phone."
If you have internal problems it is not a good idea to share the situation with your caller. Don't broadcast problems.

There are other negative telephone statements that are frequently used. You can probably list several. The point is, everything you say on the telephone influences a caller's perception of you *and* your company.

On the next page is a short exercise asking you to convert "negative customer statements" into "positive customer statements".

SOME STATEMENTS TO AVOID (continued)

Read the following statements. If you think the statement might result in a poor customer perception of your company rewrite it. Here's a tip. Imagine you are a customer hearing the statement during a call.

1. "THE SHIPPING DATE ON YOUR ORDER SHOULD BE NEXT FRIDAY."

_____

_____

2. "I'M SORRY I DIDN'T CALL YOU BACK. MY BOSS HAD US IN ANOTHER MEETING THAT LASTED ALL MORNING."

_____

_____

3. "I HOPE THIS WILL SOLVE YOUR PROBLEM."

_____

_____

4. "I DON'T UNDERSTAND WHY CUSTOMER SERVICE DIDN'T HELP YOU."

_____

_____

5. "ORDER PROCESSING HAS HAD A LOT OF PROBLEMS LATELY. I'LL CALL OVER THERE AND GET THIS STRAIGHTENED OUT FOR YOU."

_____

_____

6. "MR. KING IS IN A MEETING. WHY DON'T YOU CALL BACK IN AN HOUR?"

_____

_____

7. "I'M SORRY IT TOOK SO LONG. NOW WHAT DO YOU WANT."

_____

_____

8. "I'M SORRY YOU HAD TO WAIT. OUR TELEPHONE OPERATORS ARE VERY SLOW."

_____

_____

SOME STATEMENTS TO AVOID (continued)
(ANSWERS FROM PAGE 38)

Your phrasing does not have to be identical with the following suggestions. If your statement is positive, it is probably correct.

1. "THE SHIPPING DATE ON YOUR ORDER SHOULD BE NEXT FRIDAY."
"Your shipping date will be next Friday."

2. "I'M SORRY I DIDN'T CALL YOU BACK. MY BOSS HAD US IN ANOTHER MEETING THAT LASTED ALL MORNING."
"I'm sorry I was unable to get back to you sooner. How may I help you?" or
"Thanks for being patient. What can I do for you?"

3. "I HOPE THIS WILL SOLVE YOUR PROBLEM."
"This will solve the problem." or
"Allow me to take care of the problem"

4. "I DON'T UNDERSTAND WHY CUSTOMER SERVICE DIDN'T HELP YOU."*
"I'm sorry there has been a misunderstanding. Please hold and I'll call customer service for you. Will that be all right?"

5. "ORDER PROCESSING HAS HAD A LOT OF PROBLEMS LATELY. I'LL CALL OVER THERE AND GET THIS STRAIGHTENED OUT FOR YOU."*
"I'll be pleased to call order processing for you and resolve your problem. Do you mind holding for a minute?"

6. "MR. KING IS IN A MEETING. WHY DON'T YOU CALL BACK IN AN HOUR?"
"Mr. King is unavailable right now. May I help you?" or
"Mr. King is away from his office at the moment. May I help you or would you prefer to leave a message?"

7. "I'M SORRY IT TOOK SO LONG. NOW WHAT DO YOU WANT."
"I'm sorry that you had to wait. How may I help you?"

8. "I'M SORRY YOU HAD TO WAIT. OUR TELEPHONE OPERATORS ARE VERY SLOW."
"I'm sorry that you had to wait. How may I help you?" or
"I apologize for the delay. Normally our telephone attendants are speedy."

If you find yourself using negative words, phrases, or sentences you need to take corrective action. One simple idea is to write "POSITIVE WORDS ONLY" and tape it to your telephone. Every time you use the telephone it will serve as a reminder to communicate a positive response.

---

*Note: There are a variety of positive statements that can be made for statements 4 and 5. The correct re-phrasing should include a positive action plan for the customer.

TELEPHONE TECHNIQUE SIXTEEN: CLOSING THE CONVERSATION

When you finish your telephone conversation there are some appropriate and courteous statements that should always be made. You should:

1. Thank the customer for calling.

2. Let the customer know you appreciate his/her business.

3. Provide assurance that any promises will be fulfilled.

4. Leave the customer with a positive feeling.

SOME COURTEOUS CLOSING STATEMENT EXAMPLES:

"Thank you for calling. We appreciate your business."

"Thanks for your order."

"Feel free to call us anytime."

"I'm glad we were able to help."

"Goodbye and thanks for calling."

"I enjoyed talking with you."

"If you have any additional questions please call me."

Let the customer hang up first

This is simple courtesy, plus it gives the caller a final chance to add something.

SECTION III

UNDERSTANDING CUSTOMER NEEDS

Now that you have learned some important telephone techniques, let's concentrate on the customer. Every customer has needs and expectations that must be met. To understand these needs, carefully complete the exercises and activities in this section.

On the following page is a conversation between Mike, an order taker, and his supervisor Mary. Make note of how you would answer if your supervisor asked the same questions Mary is asking Mike.

UNDERSTANDING CUSTOMER NEEDS (continued)

As a trainee in the order processing department of the Amax, Inc., Mike's job is to answer customer telephone calls, provide price quotes, and take orders. The job is hectic because of the number of calls received each day.

After a few weeks on the job, Mike's supervisor, Mary, met with him to discuss his job performance. Mary began the discussion with a question.

Mary:	"Mike, how do you think you are doing?"
Mike:	"Well, pretty good I think. There is still a lot to learn but I feel I am making progress."
Mary:	"I agree. Your progress has been good. Let me ask you a question; How would you describe the responsibilities of your job?"
Mike:	"My responsibilities include handling as many customer calls as possible; making sure my orders are accurate; and knowing our products well."
Mary:	"Those are all important responsibilities and you are doing a good job in those areas."
Mike:	"Thanks."
Mary:	"How do you think you are at providing good customer service?"
Mike:	"I must be O.K. Since I don't know of any customer complaints."
Mary:	"I don't know of any complaints either, but what type of service do you think our customer's want?"
Mike:	"Well, I haven't thought much about it. I guess they want accurate orders and fast delivery. From what many tell me, they are not too happy with our delivery dates."

Mike has the potential to be a very good order processor, and provider of quality customer service. Right now however, Mike is like a lot of people in similar jobs. He is so busy handling customer calls that he has not had time to think about customer service.

When his supervisor asked him "What type of service do you think your customers want?" Mike did not have a clear understanding of his customer's service needs.

WHAT YOUR CUSTOMER WANTS

To better understand what your customer wants, "listen" to three customers explain their needs.

Suppose you asked three of your customers "What are your service needs?" Chances are you would hear statements similar to those that follow. As you read each response, LISTEN closely to what the customer has to say. Then write in the space provided what you think the customer wants.

CUSTOMER #1

"I want service I can depend on. When I call your company and have a question, I expect an answer. I don't want to be transferred from one person to another only to learn someone needs to call me back. I also expect correct information. If I receive incorrect information, it may cause me a lot of unnecessary work. For example, if you promise a delivery date, I want to depend on that information. When you don't do what you promised it causes problems for me."

WHAT DOES CUSTOMER # 1 WANT?

CUSTOMER # 1

1.

2.

3.

4.

WHAT YOUR CUSTOMER WANTS (continued)

CUSTOMER #2

"When we decide to buy from a company we consider everything; the product, the service and the price. Most companies have an 800 number. All promise wonderful service but sometimes I feel the only service is the 800 number. I want to speak with someone who knows what they are doing and can help me. We like consistency. We want to receive courteous, fast service from everyone with whom we speak. I hate callbacks. I know it is not possible for someone to immediately help me every time I call, but the majority of the time we should be able to get the information we need."

CUSTOMER #2 WANTS:

1.

2.

3.

4.

CUSTOMER #2 also mentioned three considerations they take into account when they decide to buy from a company.

WHAT WERE THEY?

1.

2.

3.

WHAT YOUR CUSTOMER WANTS (continued)

CUSTOMER #3

''My biggest complaint is people who don't listen. Sometimes it seems they are just going through the motions. If I call, and explain what I want, or what I think I want, they seem to simply record the information, quote a price and say goodbye. I'm sure there are times when suggestions could be offered to me about different alternatives. Customer service representatives should know their products and services better than I do. Another thing, I don't enjoy being put on hold. I often hear, ''Please hold for a second while I check that.'' Then, after what seems like an eternity, I hear a live voice again.''

CUSTOMER #3 WANTS:

1.

2.

3.

(Check your answer with the author on the next page)

WHAT YOUR CUSTOMER WANTS (continued)

AUTHOR RESPONSES

CUSTOMER NEEDS AND WANTS

CUSTOMER #1 WANTS: (PAGE 43)

1. DEPENDABLE SERVICE
2. ANSWERS TO QUESTIONS
3. NOT TO BE TRANSFERRED FROM ONE PERSON TO ANOTHER
4. CORRECT INFORMATION

CUSTOMER # 2 WANTS: (PAGE 44)

1. TO TALK WITH SOMEONE WHO KNOWS WHAT THEY ARE DOING
2. CONSISTENT SERVICE
3. COURTEOUS SERVICE
4. A FAST RESPONSE

CUSTOMER #2 SAID: WHEN WE DECIDE TO BUY FROM A COMPANY WE CONSIDER:

1. THE PRODUCT
2. THE SERVICE
3. THE PRICE

CUSTOMER #3 SAID: (PAGE 45)

1. LISTEN
2. OFFER SUGGESTIONS
3. DON'T PUT ME ON HOLD

Having completed the exercise—answer this question:

ARE THE CUSTOMERS ASKING FOR TOO MUCH?

When you think about it, customers do ask for a lot. They expect a fast response, error-free information, quality products, courteous treatment, on-time shipments, and much more.

WHAT YOUR CUSTOMER WANTS (continued)

CUSTOMER NEEDS

If you were the customer, would your needs be any different from those mentioned at the bottom of page 46? Wouldn't you expect quality service? If the company you called failed to provide what you wanted, wouldn't you do what most customers do; namely, find another company to do business with?

CUSTOMER NEED	CUSTOMER MEANING
1. LISTEN TO ME	PAY ATTENTION— UNDERSTAND ME—HEAR WHAT I HAVE TO SAY.
2. I WANT DEPENDABLE SERVICE	I NEED TO KNOW YOU WILL MEET YOUR COMMITMENTS.
3. GIVE ME CORRECT INFORMATION	DON'T GUESS AT THE RIGHT ANSWER—IF YOU DON'T KNOW OR HAVE TO CHECK, OKAY, BUT DON'T GIVE ME THE WRONG INFORMATION.
4. DO NOT TRANSFER ME FROM PERSON TO PERSON	CONNECT ME WITH THE RIGHT PERSON THE FIRST TIME. DON'T JUST GET RID OF ME. DON'T LEAVE ME ON HOLD.
5. KNOW YOUR JOB, HELP ME AND WHEN APPROPRIATE, OFFER SUGGESTIONS	I DEPEND ON YOUR KNOWLEDGE. PLEASE OFFER SUGGESTIONS OR COUNSEL ME.
6. I NEED CONSISTENT SERVICE	BE DEPENDABLE. TREAT ME LIKE THE IMPORTANT CUSTOMER I AM.
7. I EXPECT COURTEOUS SERVICE	LET ME KNOW YOU APPRECIATE MY BUSINESS EACH TIME I CALL.
8. I EXPECT ACTION	DON'T MAKE ME WAIT UNECESSARILY. I KNOW YOU CAN'T ALWAYS MEET MY DEMANDS BUT BE AS RESPONSIVE AS POSSIBLE.

ATTITUDE IS YOUR KEY TO SUCCESS

We have talked about procedures thus far, however perhaps the key factor to quality customer is your ATTITUDE.*

ATTITUDE IS YOUR MENTAL POSITION WITH REGARD TO FACTS—OR MORE SIMPLY, THE WAY YOU VIEW THINGS.

There are five important items about attitude that you should always remember.

1. YOUR ATTITUDE TOWARD CUSTOMERS INFLUENCES YOUR BEHAVIOR. YOU CANNOT ALWAYS CAMOUFLAGE HOW YOU FEEL.

2. YOUR ATTITUDE DETERMINES THE LEVEL OF YOUR JOB SATISFACTION.

3. YOUR ATTITUDE AFFECTS EVERYONE WHO COMES IN CONTACT WITH YOU, EITHER IN PERSON OR ON THE TELEPHONE.

4. YOUR ATTITUDE IS NOT ONLY REFLECTED BY YOUR TONE OF VOICE, BUT ALSO BY THE WAY YOU STAND OR SIT, YOUR FACIAL EXPRESSION; AND IN OTHER NON-VERBAL WAYS.

5. YOUR ATTITUDE IS NOT FIXED. THE ATTITUDE YOU CHOOSE TO DISPLAY IS UP TO YOU.

Whenever you talk on the telephone you have a choice. You can reflect a positive, upbeat attitude, or you can make another, less desirable, choice.

It is not always easy to be positive. There are work situations that can have negative influences on your attitude. Someone you work with may negatively impact your attitude; your workload may be heavy and produce stress; or certain customers can be demanding and even unpleasant to deal with. All of these factors affect your attitude.

---

*For an outstanding book on attitude, order Attitude: Your Most Priceless Possession, page 67.

ATTITUDE IS YOUR KEY TO SUCCESS (continued)

You have probably had days that begin with you feeling great. As the day progresses however, your feeling of well being starts to slip away. By day's end, you are glad it is over.

If you have had this experience you are normal. However, even on down days, you have some control. Your control begins when you decide that YOU are responsible for the attitude you display. When you decide to be positive and customer oriented, you have taken the first step. Your challenge is to maintain this positive attitude despite situations that take place throughout the day.

For example, suppose your first telephone contact of the day is with a very unpleasant customer? This provides you with a choice. You can allow this unpleasant situation to negatively impact your attitude for the rest of the day, or you can put the incident behind you and consciously regain a positive attitude. Every daily activity provides another ''attitude opportunity''.

It sounds easy, doesn't it? Well, as you know it is not always that easy. However, you also probably know that the benefits of a positive customer-oriented attitude outweigh the alternatives. For one thing, with a positive attitude your job satisfaction remains high, and you will continue to provide good customer service.

ATTITUDE IS YOUR KEY TO SUCCESS (continued)

Following are some thoughts to help you establish and maintain a positive and customer-oriented attitude.

1. Start each day with thoughts about the positive aspects of your job.

2. When negative events occur, take a deep breath and re-establish a positive attitude by focusing on activities that allow you to regain your perspective.

3. Whenever possible avoid people and situations that are predictably negative.

4. Share your attitude when things are going well. Attitudes are caught not taught.

JAMES RECEIVED A POOR JOB PERFORMANCE REVIEW. HIS SUPERVISOR SAID HIS ATTITUDE TOWARDS CUSTOMERS WAS THE BIGGEST PROBLEM. THIS TOOK JAMES BY SURPRISE BECAUSE HE WAS UNAWARE OF THE AFFECT HE WAS HAVING ON OTHERS.

JAMES DECIDED TO TRY TO IMPROVE HIS ATTITUDE. FIRST, HE MADE A LIST OF WHAT HE CONSIDERED TO BE NEGATIVE IMPACTS ON HIS ATTITUDE. AFTER REVIEWING THE LIST JAMES REALIZED THAT DEALING WITH TWO OR THREE UNPLEASANT CUSTOMERS EACH DAY HAD A NEGATIVE INFLUENCE ON HIS ATTITUDE TOWARDS ALL OF THE OTHERS. JAMES SUDDENLY REALIZED THAT ALTHOUGH HE TALKED WITH THIRTY CUSTOMERS A DAY HE WAS ALLOWING A VERY SMALL PERCENTAGE OF THEM TO NEGATIVELY INFLUENCE HIS BEHAVIOR.

JAMES DECIDED TO IMPROVE HIS ATTITUDE BY REFLECTING ON CUSTOMER SUCCESSES HE HAD ALREADY EXPERIENCED FOLLOWING EACH UNPLEASANT CUSTOMER EXPERIENCE.

The facing page contains a customer service attitude survey. This should provide you with feedback about your attitude towards customers.

ATTITUDE IS YOUR KEY TO SUCCESS (continued)

To check your customer service attitude, complete this survey. Answer each statement honestly.

(CIRCLE ONE)

1. T or F   CUSTOMERS EXPECT TOO MUCH FROM ME.

2. T or F   CUSTOMERS SHOULD TRY TO UNDERSTAND SOME OF OUR PROBLEMS.

3. T or F   IT IS NOT REASONABLE FOR A CUSTOMER TO EXPECT A FAST RESPONSE ON EVERY CALL.

4. T or F   CUSTOMERS ARE TOO DEPENDENT.

5. T or F   CUSTOMERS SHOULD NOT MIND BEING PLACED ON HOLD FOR A MINUTE OR SO.

6. T or F   IF CUSTOMERS KNEW HOW MANY CALLS I HANDLED EVERY DAY THEY WOULD APPRECIATE ME MORE.

7. T or F   CUSTOMERS SHOULD SHOW GREATER PATIENCE.

8. T or F   CUSTOMERS SHOULD UNDERSTAND WHY WE CAN'T HELP THEM WHEN THEY FIRST CALL.

9. T or F   CUSTOMERS ARE TOO QUICK TO ESCALATE PROBLEMS TO MY SUPERVISOR.

10. T or F   MOST CUSTOMERS SHOULD TRY AND SOLVE THEIR OWN PROBLEMS BEFORE THEY CALL US.

GIVE YOURSELF 1 POINT FOR EACH FALSE ANSWER AND 2 POINTS FOR EACH TRUE ANSWER.

YOUR SCORE: _____

(Answers are on the next page)

ATTITUDE IS YOUR KEY TO SUCCESS (continued)

All of the answers are FALSE. If you scored a perfect 10, congratulations. If you scored higher than 13, your customer service attitude could use some improvement.

Let's review why the answers are false.

Q1. Customers do expect a lot of service. As a provider of customer service it is not your job to define your customer's needs, simply to respond to those needs.

Q2. Why should the customer need to understand your problems? They are concerned with their own problems.

Q3. The customer feels it is reasonable. Customers call when their work involves your company. They do not want to wait.

Q4. Some customers become very dependent on companies they do business with. This is exactly what you want. Customers who feel comfortable calling you will become regulars.

Q5. Try this: look at the second hand on your watch then close your eyes. Keep them closed until you think a minute has elapsed, then open them. More than likely you opened your eyes before the minute was up. A minute can be a long time.

Q6. The customer doesn't really care how busy you are. Customers want to feel important. When they call they expect your full attention.

Q7. Yes, they probably should. Impatience, however, comes with the territory.

Q8. A customer wants fast, courteous service. When they have to wait, they are not getting what they want. When callbacks are unavoidable, arrange to call the customer at a specific time. Do everything possible to honor this commitment.

Q9. Some customers _are_ too quick to talk to supervisors. When they ask to do so they are saying "You are not meeting my needs and I want to talk with someone else." There will be times you cannot satisfy a customer. Discuss these situations with your supervisor to learn how they are to be handled.

Q10. Yes, some customers could avoid calling you if they tried to solve their own problems. But why should they? The customer's view is; "That's your job." Why spend time solving problems if there is a more simple way to get a solution? Be grateful when customers call.

QUALITY CUSTOMER SERVICE DEFINED

Thus far in Section III we have learned customers wants and needs; and learned the importance of a positive attitude. Now let's see if you can define what good customer service is. Write your brief definition below.

TO ME QUALITY CUSTOMER SERVICE MEANS: _____

_____

_____

_____

_____

_____

_____

There are several acceptable definitions of quality customer service. One key phrase that should always be included in a definition however is:

SATISFY CUSTOMER NEEDS

If you included this phrase (or one close to it), your answer is a good one. Following is the author's definition:

> QUALITY CUSTOMER SERVICE SATISFIES CUSTOMER NEEDS (REAL OR PERCEIVED) IN A CONSISTENT AND DEPENDABLE MANNER.

Note the phrase "REAL or PERCEIVED". This is very important in understanding quality customer service. It is not your perception of how good the service is that counts. IT IS THE CUSTOMER'S PERCEPTION, and this is discussed in the next section of this book.

SECTION IV

MANAGING THE CUSTOMER'S PERCEPTION

The final section of this book is devoted to understanding and managing customer perceptions. These perceptions includes how customers react to your attitude; your concern for their problems; and the way you handle their questions or service requirements.

When you provide service over the telephone you may speak with the same customer many times. Even though you have never met this person face to face, you probably have an idea of what he or she is like. You may even have a mental image of what a particular customer looks like. Customers are no different. They also have an image of you.

Think of your favorite radio personality. If you see them in person, or on television they often do not look like you imagined they would. The personality of their voice has created a mental image for you. Radio broadcasters are professional people. They create the image they want you to have. When you provide quality customer service, you are doing the same thing.

Let's quickly review the definition of quality customer service.

GOOD CUSTOMER SERVICE: SATISFIES CUSTOMER NEEDS (REAL OR PERCEIVED) IN A CONSISTENT AND DEPENDABLE MANNER.

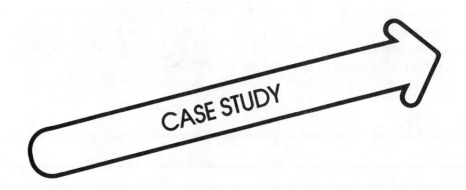

CASE STUDY

CASE STUDY: THE WHOLESALE WIDGET COMPANY

You are Customer Service Manager of the Wholesale Widget Company. You believe customer service is good because there have been very few customer complaints. The company is profitable and sales have been increasing. Despite this you feel a survey of customers would be worthwhile to learn their feelings about WWC's service. A few weeks ago, you mailed several hundred customer service questionnaires.

> THE RESULTS WERE:
>
> 62% RATED YOUR CUSTOMER SERVICE "AVERAGE"
>
> 23% RATED IT "POOR"
>
> 13% RATED IT "GOOD"
>
> 2% RATED IT "EXCELLENT"

With these results, what attitude best reflects your thinking as Customer Service Manager?

1. 77% of our customers rated our service as average or better. That's pretty good.

2. Our average customer is satisfied. Overall we need some improvement but we are doing a pretty good job.

3. We have a serious problem. 23% of our customers rated our service as poor. We need to do something, and do it now!

A. Which statement reflects your view? _____ #1 _____ #2 or _____#3.

B. List three steps you will take to improve customer service.

    1.

    2.

    3.

C. If this situation is not corrected, list three things that could happen to your company?

    1.

    2.

    3.

TURN THE PAGE FOR THE ANSWERS

CASE STUDY: AUTHOR'S RESPONSE

A. WHICH STATEMENT REFLECTS YOUR VIEW?

The best answer is #3. We have a serious problem. Whenever customers are dissatisfied with service something must be done. In this case, a very high percentage (23%) are dissatisfied. Prior to the survey you thought service was good. You were wrong. It is customers who decide how good the service is.

B. WHAT STEPS SHOULD BE TAKEN?

The first thing you need to do is find out why your customers are not satisfied. Next, a plan should be developed to address specific customer concerns. Finally, it will be necessary to implement and monitor this plan.

Your answer should be similar to the above. As customer service manager you will need a method for customer feedback to insure your plan is working.

C. IF YOUR SERVICE SITUATION IS NOT CORRECTED WHAT COULD HAPPEN TO THE COMPANY?

When customers are not satisfied they will take their business elsewhere. Sales will fall and profits will tumble. Customers will mention their poor experience to others, and the reputation of the company will suffer. Ultimately there will be fewer jobs, smaller pay increases, and less opportunity for all.

RATE THE CUSTOMER'S PERCEPTION

THE CUSTOMER'S PERCEPTION: AN EXERCISE

Following is a list of telephone statements that have been made to customers. Read each statement and rate the "PERCEPTION" you think a customer would have after hearing the statement. Rate each statement with a "G" if you think the customer reaction would be good; and a "P" if you think it would be poor.

RATING

1. _____ GOOD MORNING, WHOLESALE WIDGET COMPANY, JIM SMITH SPEAKING. MAY I HELP YOU?

2. _____ SORRY THAT'S NOT MY JOB...YOU WILL HAVE TO CALL THE ORDER PROCESSING DEPARTMENT.

3. _____ GOOD MORNING, WHOLESALE WIDGET.

4. _____ MRS. JONES IS OUT. ANY MESSAGE?

5. _____ THANKS FOR YOUR ORDER.

6. _____ I DON'T WORK IN THAT DEPARTMENT SO I CAN'T HELP YOU.

7. _____ GOOD MORNING, CUSTOMER SERVICE.

8. _____ I REALLY DON'T KNOW WHY OUR SERVICE PERSON DIDN'T RETURN YOUR CALL. DID YOU TRY AND CALL THEM BACK?

9. _____ I'M SORRY IT TOOK SO LONG TO GET BACK TO YOU. I'M SURE WE CAN SOLVE YOUR PROBLEM WITH THIS CALL. NOW, HOW MAY I HELP YOU?

10. _____ MAY I REVIEW YOUR ORDER TO INSURE SURE WE HAVE ALL OF THE INFORMATION?

11. _____ WHO WERE YOU HOLDING FOR?

12. _____ THANKS FOR CALLING.

13. _____ MR. SMITH I'M SORRY YOU RECEIVED THE WRONG MATERIAL BUT I WROTE THE ORDER DOWN JUST AS YOU GAVE IT TO ME.

AUTHOR RESPONSE TO THE CUSTOMER'S PERCEPTION EXERCISE

1. **Good morning, Wholesale Widget Company Jim Smith speaking. May I help you?**
   PERCEPTION RATING: GOOD. THE TELEPHONE WAS ANSWERED USING THE FOUR COURTESY POINTS.
   1. A GREETING   2. STATEMENT OF COMPANY NAME
   3. THE PERSON'S NAME   4. AN OFFER OF HELP
   If an incoming call has been previously answered at a central station there is no need to restate the company name. In this case the department or group name should be used.

2. **Sorry, that's not my job…you will have to call the order processing department.**
   PERCEPTION RATING: POOR. THIS STATEMENT WILL ONLY FRUSTRATE THE CUSTOMER.

3. **Good morning, Wholesale Widget.**
   PERCEPTION RATING: POOR. IF A RECEPTIONIST MADE THIS STATEMENT IT WOULD BE ACCEPTABLE IF AN OFFER TO HELP WAS INCLUDED. IN TELEPHONE SITUATIONS, WHERE A CALL IS ANSWERED AT A CENTRAL POINT AND THEN ROUTED TO THE REQUESTED INDIVIDUAL OR DEPARTMENT THERE IS NO NEED FOR A PERSONAL INTRODUCTION. IN ALL OTHER CASES HOWEVER IT IS IMPORTANT TO LET THE CUSTOMER KNOW TO WHOM THEY ARE SPEAKING.

4. **Mrs. Jones is out. Any message?**
   PERCEPTION RATING: POOR. IF YOU CHANGE THE PHRASE TO: MAY I TAKE A MESSAGE? IT WOULD BE MORE ACCEPTABLE.

5. **Thanks for your order.**
   PERCEPTION RATING: GOOD. THIS SIMPLE STATEMENT SHOULD ALWAYS BE USED WHEN THE CUSTOMER PLACES AN ORDER.

6. **I don't work in that department so I can't help you.**
   PERCEPTION RATING: POOR. EVEN THOUGH YOU DO NOT WORK IN THAT DEPARTMENT AND CANNOT HELP THE CUSTOMER, THERE IS NO EXCUSE FOR NOT OFFERING TO HELP BY TRANSFERRING THE CALL OR TAKING A MESSAGE.

7. **Good morning, customer service.**
PERCEPTION RATING: POOR. TWO OF THE FOUR CUSTOMER
ANSWERING COURTESY POINTS WERE OMITTED:
   1. INTRODUCING YOURSELF
   2. OFFERING TO HELP

8. **I really don't know why our service person didn't return your call. Did you try to call them back?**
PERCEPTION RATING: POOR. TO PROVIDE GOOD SERVICE MEANS
TAKING RESPONSIBILITY. THIS DOES NOT MEAN YOU HAVE TO
PERSONALLY SOLVE THE CUSTOMER'S PROBLEM BUT YOU NEED TO
ASSURE THE CUSTOMER CORRECTIVE ACTION WILL BE TAKEN.

9. **I'm sorry it took so long to get back to you. I'm sure we can solve your problem with this call. Now, how may I help you?**
PERCEPTION RATING: GOOD. AN APOLOGY WAS MADE FOR SLOW
SERVICE AND THE CUSTOMER RECEIVED ASSURANCE THAT THE
PROBLEM WILL BE SOLVED.

10. **May I review your order to insure we have all the information?**
PERCEPTION RATING: GOOD. ACCURACY IS IMPORTANT. TO QUICKLY
REPEAT A CUSTOMER'S ORDER OR REQUEST IS A GOOD IDEA.

11. **Who were you holding for?**
PERCEPTION RATING: POOR. NOT KNOWING WHO THE CUSTOMER IS
HOLDING FOR IS A COMMON PROBLEM. WHEN THIS OCCURS, GET ON
THE LINE AND SAY: I'M SORRY, I HAVE FORGOTTEN WHO YOU WERE
HOLDING FOR. THEN WRITE THE PERSON'S NAME SO YOU WILL
REMEMBER. WHENEVER POSSIBLE PROVIDE THE CALLER WITH A
STATUS REPORT. FOR EXAMPLE: "SALLY IS STILL ON ANOTHER CALL.
WOULD YOU LIKE TO CONTINUE TO HOLD OR MAY I TAKE YOUR
NUMBER AND HAVE HER CALL YOU?" WHENEVER POSSIBLE GIVE THE
CUSTOMER A CHOICE.

12. **Thanks for calling.**
PERCEPTION RATING: GOOD. ALWAYS THANK A CUSTOMER FOR
CALLING.

13. **Mr. Smith I'm sorry you received the wrong material but I wrote the order down just as you gave it to me.**
PERCEPTION RATING: POOR. WHEN A MISUNDERSTANDING OR
MISTAKE HAS OCCURRED IT IS NOT IMPORTANT TO FIX BLAME FOR THE
PROBLEM. THE IMPORTANT THING IS TO TAKE WHATEVER CORRECTIVE
ACTION IS REQUIRED TO SATISFY THE CUSTOMER.

> Every statement you make on a telephone to a customer carries with it a perception. Your objective is to manage this perception to insure there is customer satisfaction with the service your provide.

MANAGING THE CUSTOMER'S PERCEPTION: THE CUSTOMER SERVICE CALL

MARTHA:	"Good Morning, Customer Service Department, Martha English speaking. May I help you?"
CUSTOMER:	"This is Ken Taylor from AP Systems. I need to order some new valves for our engineering department."
MARTHA:	"I'll be glad to handle that for you. What type do you need?"
CUSTOMER:	"Well, the engineering department said they needed either the 516 or the 311 models. I'm not sure which one is the best. Is there a price difference?"
MARTHA:	"Yes, there is a 50 cent difference. The 516 is less expensive. How many valves do you need?"
CUSTOMER:	"We need 85."
MARTHA:	"Do you mind holding while I work up a price quote?"
CUSTOMER:	"No go right ahead."
MARTHA:	"Thanks for holding. The price on the 516 is $2.00 per valve. The 311's are $2.50 each. Your total cost for the 516 would be $170.00, and $212.50 for the 311. Would you like me to explain the difference between the two models?"
CUSTOMER:	"Yes, please do."
MARTHA:	"The 516 is our newer design. It is stronger and a little smaller than the 311. I think the last time your company ordered they purchased the 516. Would you like me to check on that?"
CUSTOMER:	"Yes, would you please."
MARTHA:	"Sure. Do you mind holding for a moment?"
CUSTOMER:	"No."
MARTHA:	"I'll be right back."
MARTHA:	"Thanks for holding. Your last order was in June and you ordered the 516."

CUSTOMER: "I had better double check with engineering. I will have to call you right back."

MARTHA: "If you like I'll hold while you call them. Will that be okay?"

CUSTOMER: "Sure, I'll be right back."

CUSTOMER: "I'm glad I checked. They want the 311."

MARTHA: "So that will be eight-five 311 valves. Is the billing and shipping address the same as your last order."

CUSTOMER: "Yes it is."

MARTHA: "Good, we will get the shipment out this afternoon and you can expect delivery on Friday. Will that be all right?"

CUSTOMER: "Yes, that's fine."

MARTHA: "Is there anything else I can do for you?"

CUSTOMER: "No, that should do it."

MARTHA: "Thanks for your order."

CUSTOMER: "You're welcome. Goodbye."

MARTHA: "Goodbye."

In this telephone contact Martha provided the customer with excellent service. The customer appeared unsure about which valve to order. Martha helped by explaining the differences; by checking on a previous order; and then holding while her customer checked with engineering. Martha was patient and offered every assistance she could.

Let's examine a few of Martha's statements to see the customer perception they provided.

MANAGING THE CUSTOMER
PERCEPTION (continued)

MARTHA'S STATEMENTS	CUSTOMER'S PERCEPTION
"Good morning, Order Processing Department. Martha English speaking. How may I help you?"	SHE IS FRIENDLY AND WANTS TO HELP US.
"Do you mind holding while I work up a price quote?"	SHE IS COURTEOUS.
"I think the last time your company ordered they purchased the 516. Would you like me to check that for you?"	SHE IS OFFERING HER ASSISTANCE.
"Do you mind holding for a few seconds."	SHE ASKS PERMISSION BEFORE PLACING THE CUSTOMER ON HOLD.
"If you want I'll hold while you call them. (engineering) Will that be all right?	SHE IS CONCERNED—WANTS TO HELP—PROVIDES COURTEOUS SERVICE
"Is there anything else I can do for you?"	SHE OFFERS ADDITIONAL HELP.
"Thanks for your order."	SHE APPRECIATES MY BUSINESS.

Suppose you were the customer. What do you think your perception of Martha and her company would be? How would you rate the customer service she provided? Check each statement below that you think her customer Ken Taylor would agree with.

1. ___ I can depend on their service.   ___ 6. I was counseled.

2. ___ I received a fast response.   ___ 7. I received courteous service.

3. ___ I can trust their service.   ___ 8. The information was accurate.

4. ___ Martha was very helpful.   ___ 9. She understood my problem.

5. ___ She listened to me.   ___ 10. I can rely on them.

Ken probably would have checked all of the statements. In one simple telephone conversation the needs of the customer were completely met.

TELEPHONE SERVICE SKILLS INVENTORY

The kind of service you provide is up to you. If your objective is to become a professional customer service provider, two things must be done. First you need to assess your present skill level to determine where improvement is needed. Next you need to develop a personal action plan to improve your skills. These steps can be done using this page and the "Action Plan" on page 66, with the help of your supervisor.

Following is a service skills inventory. Grade yourself on each skill area. Use a rating of "A" if you feel you are excellent at the particular skill, "B" for good, and "C" if you need improvement. Ask your supervisor to provide his/her opinion on your self-scored assessments.

SERVICE

_____ I accept responsibility for providing customer service

_____ I understand the importance of quality service

_____ I know what our customer's want and need

_____ I satisfy customers by understanding their needs and doing my job well

_____ I realize that a positive customer perception of our service is essential

_____ I am customer oriented

_____ I have a positive attitude

TELEPHONE TECHNIQUES: I know how to:

_____ handle the telephone and use all of its features

_____ extend courtesy on every call

_____ address the caller

_____ transmit a positive attitude

_____ answer calls using the four courtesies

_____ listen to distinguish between statements, objections, and questions

_____ manage objections

_____ ask questions. (I know how and when to use open and closed questions and can question to determine problems and requests)

_____ make outbound calls

_____ deliver bad news—(I can use the two techniques)

_____ recognize & manage caller behavior—(I know how to manage the aggressive and assertive callers)

_____ arrange customer callbacks—(I always make and keep commitments)

_____ Avoid using statements that will create the wrong customer perception

---

Develop a personal action plan for better service on the next page.

YOUR ACTION PLAN FOR BETTER SERVICE

Your personal action plan will be developed in four steps:

STEP 1.   List all skill areas you rated as ''B'' or ''C''.

_____

_____

_____

_____

_____

STEP 2.   Identify your five most critical skill areas that need improvement.

1. _____   2. _____   3. _____

4. _____   5. _____

STEP 3.   Write down an action plan to improve the five skills. Include specific activities and dates you plan to start and complete, (use a separate piece of paper for this step).

SKILL AREA	IMPROVEMENT ACTIVITY	START	COMPLETE
1. _____	_____	_____	_____
2. _____	_____	_____	_____
3. _____	_____	_____	_____
4. _____	_____	_____	_____
5. _____	_____	_____	_____

STEP 4:   Review Steps 1, 2 and 3 with your supervisor and commit to a date to review progress on your action plan.

Once you have made progress with the first five skill areas you can develop an action plan for any remaining skill areas rated ''B'' or ''C''. Maintain a personal action plan until you rate an ''A'' in each skill area. When your ratings are all ''A's'' you have reached your objective of becoming a provider of quality customer service. Make a commitment to yourself to become a professional. Good luck!

ABOUT THE FIFTY-MINUTE SERIES

''Every so often an idea emerges that is so simple and appealing, people wonder why it didn't come along sooner. The Fifty-Minute series is just such an idea. Excellent!''

**Mahaliah Levine, Vice President for
Training and Development
Dean Witter Reynolds, Inc.**

WHAT IS A FIFTY-MINUTE BOOK?

—Fifty-Minute books are brief, soft-covered, ''self-study'' titles covering a wide variety of topics pertaining to business and self-improvement. They are reasonably priced, ideal for formal training, excellent for self-study and perfect for remote location training.

''A Fifty-Minute book gives the reader fundamentals that can be applied on the job, even before attending a formal class''

**Lynn Baker, Manager of Training
Fleming Corporation**

WHY ARE FIFTY-MINUTE BOOKS UNIQUE?

—Because of their format. Designed to be ''read with a pencil,'' the basics of a subject can be quickly grasped and applied through a series of hands-on activities, exercises and cases.

''Fifty-Minute books are the best new publishing idea in years. They are clear, practical, concise and affordable—perfect for today's world.''

**Leo Hauser, Past President
ASTD**

HOW MANY FIFTY-MINUTE BOOKS ARE THERE?

—Those listed on the following pages at this time. Additional titles are always in development. For more information write to **Crisp Publications, Inc.,**
95 First Street, Los Altos, CA 94022.

THE FIFTY-MINUTE SERIES

Quantity	Title	Code #	Price	Amount
	MANAGEMENT TRAINING			
	Successful Negotiation	09-2	$7.95	
	Personal Performance Contracts	12-2	$7.95	
	Team Building	16-5	$7.95	
	Effective Meeting Skills	33-5	$7.95	
	An Honest Day's Work	39-4	$7.95	
	Managing Disagreement Constructively	41-6	$7.95	
	Training Managers To Train	43-2	$7.95	
	The Fifty-Minute Supervisor	58-0	$7.95	
	Leadership Skills For Women	62-9	$7.95	
	Problem Solving & Decision Making	63-7	$7.95	
	Coaching & Counseling For Supervisors	68-8	$7.95	
	Management Dilemmas: A Guide to Business Ethics	69-6	$7.95	
	Understanding Organizational Change	71-8	$7.95	
	Project Management	75-0	$7.95	
	Managing Organizational Change	80-7	$7.95	
	Managing A Diverse Workforce	85-8	$7.95	
	PERSONNEL TRAINING & HUMAN RESOURCE MANAGEMENT			
	Effective Performance Appraisals	11-4	$7.95	
	Quality Interviewing	13-0	$7.95	
	Personal Counseling	14-9	$7.95	
	Job Performance and Chemical Dependency	27-0	$7.95	
	New Employee Orientation	46-7	$7.95	
	Professional Excellence for Secretaries	52-1	$7.95	
	Guide To Affirmative Action	54-8	$7.95	
	Writing A Human Resource Manual	70-X	$7.95	
	COMMUNICATIONS			
	Effective Presentation Skills	24-6	$7.95	
	Better Business Writing	25-4	$7.95	
	The Business of Listening	34-3	$7.95	
	Writing Fitness	35-1	$7.95	
	The Art of Communicating	45-9	$7.95	
	Technical Presentation Skills	55-6	$7.95	
	Making Humor Work For You	61-0	$7.95	
	Better Technical Writing	64-5	$7.95	
	Using Visual Aids in Business	77-7	$7.95	
	Influencing Others: A Practical Guide	84-X	$7.95	
	SELF-MANAGEMENT			
	Balancing Home And Career	10-6	$7.95	
	Mental Fitness: A Guide to Emotional Health	15-7	$7.95	
	Personal Financial Fitness	20-3	$7.95	
	Attitude: Your Most Priceless Possession	21-1	$7.95	
	Personal Time Management	22-X	$7.95	

(Continued on next page)

THE FIFTY-MINUTE SERIES

Quantity	Title	Code #	Price	Amount
	SELF-MANAGEMENT (CONTINUED)			
	Preventing Job Burnout	23-8	$7.95	
	Successful Self-Management	26-2	$7.95	
	Developing Positive Assertiveness	38-6	$7.95	
	Time Management And The Telephone	53-X	$7.95	
	Memory Skills In Business	56-4	$7.95	
	Developing Self-Esteem	66-1	$7.95	
	Creativity In Business	67-X	$7.95	
	Quality Awareness: A Personal Guide To Professional Standards	72-6	$7.95	
	Managing Personal Change	74-2	$7.95	
	Speedreading For Better Productivity	78-5	$7.95	
	Winning At Human Relations	86-6	$7.95	
	Stop Procrastinating	88-2	$7.95	
	SALES TRAINING/QUALITY CUSTOMER SERVICE			
	Sales Training Basics	02-5	$7.95	
	Restaurant Server's Guide	08-4	$7.95	
	Quality Customer Service	17-3	$7.95	
	Telephone Courtesy And Customer Service	18-1	$7.95	
	Professional Selling	42-4	$7.95	
	Customer Satisfaction	57-2	$7.95	
	Telemarketing Basics	60-2	$7.95	
	Calming Upset Customers	65-3	$7.95	
	Managing A Quality Service Organization	83-1	$7.95	
	ENTREPRENEURSHIP			
	Marketing Your Consulting Or Professional Services	40-8	$7.95	
	Starting Your Small Business	44-0	$7.95	
	Publicity Power	82-3	$7.95	
	CAREER GUIDANCE & STUDY SKILLS			
	Study Skills Strategies	05-X	$7.95	
	Career Discovery	07-6	$7.95	
	Plan B: Protecting Your Career From The Winds of Change	48-3	$7.95	
	I Got The Job!	59-9	$7.95	
	OTHER CRISP INC. BOOKS			
	Comfort Zones: A Practical Guide For Retirement Planning	00-9	$13.95	
	Stepping Up To Supervisor	11-8	$13.95	
	The Unfinished Business Of Living: Helping Aging Parents	19-X	$12.95	
	Managing Performance	23-7	$18.95	
	Be True To Your Future: A Guide to Life Planning	47-5	$13.95	
	Up Your Productivity	49-1	$10.95	
	How To Succeed In A Man's World	79-3	$7.95	
	Practical Time Management	275-4	$13.95	
	Copyediting: A Practical Guide	51-3	$18.95	

THE FIFTY-MINUTE SERIES
(Continued)

☐ Send volume discount information.

☐ Please send me a catalog.

	Amount
Total (from other side)	
Shipping ($1.50 first book, $.50 per title thereafter)	
California Residents add 7% tax	
Total	

Ship to: _____

_____

_____

_____

Phone number: _____

Bill to: _____

_____

_____

_____

P.O. # _____

All orders except those with a P.O.# must be prepaid.
For more information Call (415) 949-4888 or FAX (415) 949-1610.